QUICK CASH IDEAS FOR SALONS

CATHERINE R BOOTH

DEDICATION

To Samantha Haddad, my encourager, Jackie Young, my
ENFP by injection, Joel, my editor, and to Leah, Kara,
Shirley and Sadie, my awesome salon team;
Thank you.

INTRODUCTION

Every now and then, when running our salons, we need a
quick cash injection to improve cashflow.

This short book is jam-packed with quick tips to bring in
that extra cash.

The focus is on speed, minimum time and product, and ease
of upsell.

ABOUT THE AUTHOR

Catherine bought a salon a few years ago and built it up into a successful, profitable salon turning over six figures a year.

She is writing a series of short books addressing common issues within small business, presenting simple solutions in condensed, easy to absorb informational books. The focus is on incremental, easy to implement improvements within business systems.

ANALYSE YOUR PROFITABLE TIMES

Zero in on the profitable hours. Do an analysis of your busy and slow periods and put more staff on the busy periods, while taking staff off the slow periods.

Consider adding nightshifts and Sunday shifts for a premium to busy clients at popular times.

INCREASING APPOINTMENT FREQUENCY

Introduce between appointment refreshers – colours and balayage. These take a shorter time than regular appointments, and while cheaper than full appointments, they still make more money per hour and increase the frequency of appointments.

What person doesn't need a reason to relax in the salon more often?

THREE
GIVE YOURSELF A PAY RISE

Raise prices – 5 or 10% across the board. This gives you an effective pay rise of 5 or 10% per week. This can be done anytime, but most salons do it at Easter, end of financial year, Christmas, or the New Year. Supermarkets do it all year round, why can't you? It's easier to create specials that still make you money if your regular prices are higher!

FOUR
TIER PRICING FOR SERVICES AND STYLISTS

Introduce tier pricing structures – highest price for the most experienced stylist, middle price for the next most experienced, and a lower price still for the apprentice or freshly graduated stylist. This three-tier system works well, and if the lower tiers are booked out, the more experienced stylists can help out at the reduced prices as a bonus to the clients.

FLASH SALES

Introduce time sensitive sales for services and products. 24-hour flash sales are highly effective, and if done regularly on different products or services, can become the highlight of the week on your salon website or page.

SIX

PSYCH UP YOUR RETAIL SALES

Don't recommend just one product. Retail psychology studies show that recommending up to three products increases the chances that the client will buy at least one product. Ensure the client handles the products at some point. It's ideal to show the client the product while doing their hair service; ask them to hold it while continuing the hair service and chatting about the product and why you're recommending it. Encourage them to open it and smell it. Explain how to use it and how much to use.

Studies show that if a client purchases a product, they are much more likely to return. The more products you sell, the higher your client retention is!

KEEP THEM COMING BACK

Add a loyalty program. A loyalty card that's punched for each visit and has a special reward on the fifth and tenth visit works well. If you have a subscription service, you could implement a reward system for signing up as well.

UPSELL YOUR LIFE

Suggest upsells to clients such as hair treatments, facials, eyebrow shaping or tinting, quick things that take little or no time and can be implemented easily at the shampoo basin or in the chair. Look at the different skills your stylists may possess and see which can be implemented into quick add on services. You could offer a concierge service where the client receives an arm and hand massage from the apprentice. Just a few upsells in a day can increase your daily take by $100 or more!

Set a goal for your team members to add at least one extra service to each appointment booked, then reward them for doing so.

Consider popping upgrade menus on salon mirrors or as

website booking software pop-up suggestions – upsell without effort! Studies show this can improve the upsell rate on up to 30% of clientele!

DOUBLE YOUR CLIENTELE

Run a special offer - bring a friend and receive a percentage or dollar amount off their service or products. This is great for slow periods. Consider running a 'Mummy and Me' day or a 'Recover from the School Holidays with a Friend' day.

TEN

EXPAND YOUR PRODUCT OPTIONS

Consider stocking a niche product within your salon. Look at your clients and see what they tend to have in common. One salon I know of sells paintings of horses to clients as they're in horse country. Another salon near a university sells classic literature in an attractive bookcase.

If you can't or don't want to source niche products locally, check out Alibaba or Ali Express to obtain bulk items such as clips or combs with your branding on to resell at a massive mark-up.

ELEVEN
CAPTURE YOUR CLIENT'S ATTENTION

If you are able, consider bringing in Tupperware, linen, makeup, lingerie or similar party plan books to the salon and watch semi-passive income grow. You could even have parties in the salon and use those parties to cross-promote your salon to potential future clients.

TWELVE
BUY ONE GET ONE FREE

Have a gift voucher sale. When I need a quick cash injection, I will have either a 'buy one voucher get one free to the same value', or a 'buy one get 50% value free' promotion. Either clients will buy for themselves to get discounted services, or they will buy for other people who can become new clients.

THIRTEEN
CLASS THINGS UP

Run hair care or skin care classes. For example, we hold a straightening hair class every month and it's always booked out. We have four chairs so we limit numbers to four clients, and one stylist can run this class. It's also a great way to sell straighteners if you can demonstrate your in-salon straighteners and show how they cut the time it takes in half every morning when they do their hair before work or school. Another great class we run is in school holidays, it's a parent-child braiding class, for that we have four parents and four children or teenagers. We make it fun with nibbles and drinks. A beauty salon could do a class on daily skin care, for example, and upsell products as well.

FOURTEEN
INTRODUCE TEAM COMPETITIONS

These can be competitions for anything. The team member with the highest daily take average per week or month, or the team member with the highest number of retail sales, or the team member with the highest number of rebookings. Prizes can be gift vouchers, experiences or beautiful items. Make it fun and consider your individual staff member's particular hobbies and likings when considering the prizes.

Perhaps have a team prize such as going out for dinner together, and then an individual prize!

CREATE VALUE ADDED PACKAGES

Look at your most popular services and consider packaging them together to provide value to your clients and improve upsells automatically. For example, our most popular sales items are trims, root colour refreshing, and eyebrow waxing. So we created a few tiers of packages—trim plus wax, a root colour refresh plus trim and wax, and so on. Include items that don't take much time or money such as basic basin treatments and eyebrow or eyelash tinting.

SIXTEEN
OFFER A FREE GIFT

Choose one or two of your most popular services that makes you decent profit and offer a free gift for each booking made within a certain time period. You can link this to a celebration such as the salon anniversary, a team member's birthday, Valentine's Day. The gift item can be anything—choose something you'd love to receive. Go to a variety store such as Kmart, Walmart or Ikea and have a look around for something AMAZING for just a couple of dollars and buy a bagful or two. Look on Alibaba or AliExpress for headscarves or makeup bags, etc., for gifts. If your focus is on gaining new clients, you can choose not to attach a service booking requirement and just tell people to come into the salon to receive a FREE gift – no obligation attached! Consumer psychology shows that receiving a gift increases the likelihood that the client will want to reciprocate by booking a service, either right there and then or later on when they need one.

BRING IN A PREPAID SYSTEM

Consider bringing in a prepaid system where clients prepay for a certain number of visits for a service or package. Bring them in by offering a free visit in return. Promote the convenience of prepaying, they just book ahead every four or six weeks or however often they like to come in and they just come in and get their service and walk out without having to spend time at reception paying. You could also offer unlimited blow-dries for a certain prepaid amount for a certain length of time. People love prepaid and subscription services. Just look at how Netflix has taken off.

RENT OUT SPARE SPACE

If you have room or a chair that is usually empty, consider renting it out to a compatible service. For example, in a beauty salon, a masseuse could take up an empty room. In a hair salon, a stylist could rent a chair or a nail technician could rent a corner of the salon. They can have their own payment structures and book their own appointments. Make that dead space work for you!

NINETEEN
APPLY FOR BUSINESS GRANTS

Governments and Councils often have grants available for small businesses to provide cash injections for specific projects. Google 'business grants' in your council area, state and country to find these. For the larger grants, it may be worth hiring a professional grant writer to apply for these.

TWENTY
VENDING MACHINES

This depends on the type of ambience your salon has as to the type of vending machine you might consider. You can hire coffee machines, soft drink can dispensers, slushy or snow cone machines and so on. If your salon has a party vibe then the snow cone machine would be a winner. For a quieter, more relaxed salon, a coffee machine might be the way to go. Some vending machine companies offer a trial period where you can try it out and analyse the cost vs profit.

TWENTY-ONE
CASHING IN ON DOWNTIME

If your salon is closed in the evenings or on Sundays, you might think of hiring out the space for things like yoga or craft classes. Of course this would mean you'd need to be able to lock away valuables and accessories.

TWENTY-TWO
SELLING ON COMMISSION

Maybe someone local to you has small handcrafted items they can sell on commission through your salon such as jewellery, scarves or headbands. Small woodwork items such as toy trucks and such do well as well. I've sold handcrafted candles quite successfully through my salon.

TWENTY-THREE
HAVE A KID'S DAY

I've had Kid's Days where I have had a face painter come in and discounted children's cuts. They get their face painted free after their haircut, and the mums can browse the products you have for sale while waiting for their child. This works well in school holidays. Don't forget to calculate the cost of the face painter in;you could always exchange services instead of cash.

TWENTY-FOUR
CASH IN ON EXPERTISE

Do you or one of your team members have special expertise in a particular area? Can you run a workshop for other professionals in your salon for that particular expertise? This can be highly lucrative as professional skill set coaching is in high demand.

DIVERSIFY YOUR SERVICES

If you have a salon, you have the ability to run another service business using the same phone and address. For example, you can create a cleaning or car detailing business and hire on call casuals. Choose a secondary business that requires minimal initial cash outlay.

HAVE SURCHARGES

Add surcharges to your price list for extra long or thick or curly hair. These take longer and use more product, so it doesn't make sense not to add on a cost to cover extra time and product.

SELL OLD STOCK

Identify old stock that hasn't sold and put a big discount on it(maybe 50%)and place an ad on Gumtree or Craigslist for them. Place at the reception desk in a bargain bucket or similar if you can.

HOLD A BRAINSTORMING MEETING

Finally, the best ideas you can get can come from your fabulous team! Hold a brainstorming meeting and write down all their ideas, no matter how crazy. Then ask each of them to choose an idea and give them the responsibility of implementing that idea and working out how it will work.

This has always been fun for my own team! I'm completely open about my goals for the salon and their role in achieving these goals; I tell them where we are at financially, and where I'd like us to be.

CUTTING COSTS

An underused way of improving profits, cutting costs carefully in ways that don't impact clients consciously are an effective way of increasing your gap between your expenditure and your profit. Stop and think... what ways come to the front of your mind that can save money in the business?

Just remember not to impact the client experience or stress the staff unduly and you'll be onto a winner!

Here are some tips to get you started cutting costs and increasing profits.

CHECK YOUR BILLS

Go over your regular bills and service providers. Ring around and see if you can get a better deal on services such as electricity, phone, bank cash machine providers and so on. Talk to your sales representative for your products and see if they can offer you discounts—usually in exchange for a minimum guaranteed order each month. I do this on one day each year and generally save around $1000 – $5000 per year by shopping around!

CANCEL SUBSCRIPTIONS

Look carefully at your magazine, television and radio or music subscriptions. Could you replace them with something free that benefits clients as much or more? Are they distracting your clients from your salon products and services? Could you replace them with magazines or video that directly support your sales? Supermarkets and chemist warehouses tend to have free magazines that are just as good as the paid subscription magazines. You could fill a USB stick with interesting videos about your products and services, your sales representative may be able to provide these. What ideas do you have?

CALL UP LAPSED CLIENTS

This is something stylists can do in downtimes. Make a list of clients that haven't come in for two months or more and call them. Just let them know you've missed them, that you hope everything is ok, and that you're looking forward to seeing them next time.

When we do this we average about two appointments made every ten calls. Often it's just slipped the client's mind that they're due for an appointment or they just needed to feel special; it's better that you make them feel special than for them to go to another salon to find that feeling that so many salons make the mistake of only offering to first time clients. Make them feel special, missed and appreciated ALL THE TIME!

RENT OUT ADVERTISING SPACE

If you have a lot of local followers on your social media or a spare shop frontage, you can rent out that space to other compatible advertisers.

For example a nail salon or masseuse may want your hair salon to promote them on your Facebook page or put a corflute poster up on your shopfront directing clients where they might find their service.

TRAIN YOUR TEAM

Instead of spending time and money on recruiting new staff with new skill sets, consider training your existing team members in the new skill sets you require. This has the double benefit of saving you time and money on recruitment costs, AND keeping your existing team members engaged, interested and happy. Invest in your existing staff! Involve them by asking them what skills they think would add to the salon's earnings and which interest them. Then send them off to school!

TIME STACKING

Stack your client appointments so while one client's hair or facial is processing, another client is being attended to in whatever service fits within the time frame. It's cheaper to hire an apprentice or junior to do the entry level jobs such as cleaning chemical pots, sweeping the floor, doing basin work, answering the phone or working reception and the salon software.

REDUCE WASTAGE

Consider bringing specialised chemical mix scales into the salon to mix products exactly without waste; set specific mass of colour for each length and thickness of hair for the team to follow. Wash chemical pots at the end of the day instead of through the day to reduce water waste. Turn off lights and appliances that aren't in use. Keep air conditioners on the recommended setting as long as it's comfortable for the clients. Boil only the cup of water that is needed in the kettle, instead of a full kettle for one cup; or consider bringing in a coffee and tea machine that heats exactly the amount of water you need. Turn off the fridge over holiday periods when you're closed for more than a day or two. Compare the price of washing reusable towels and cloths as opposed to disposable ones over the same period of time.

THIRTY-SEVEN
ORDER ONLY WHAT YOU NEED

Sales representatives often offer package deals that have great prices but include products you can't shift easily. Try to resist the hard sell and focus only on the products you can sell quickly and easily. Use tracking analysis software to show you what sells, how often, and when, so you can pace your orders accordingly. Shop smart!

DECORATING COSTS

Is it really necessary to paint the whole salon? Can you get the same fresh look by simply painting borders or an accent wall? Do you really need to replace ALL the chairs or just the tatty ones? Does the salon just need a really good deep clean? Is the landlord willing to provide you with the paint and even the painters?

ADS AND ADVERTISING

Do you track your ads? Can you tell which ads convert easily and which don't? Remove the ads that aren't performing or aren't trackable and stick with the ads that are proven performers. Ad spend can be one of a business's biggest costs, so cutting this effectively can have a real positive effect.

Try cutting one ad at a time so you can see if there's a revenue drop corresponding to that ad, rather than cutting a whole heap at a time and not knowing which one might have contributed to a sudden revenue drop.

STAFF COSTS

Analyse your cost and profit per hour per staff member on an individual basis. Can you offer the most productive one more hours and the least productive one less hours? Do you really need two juniors or would one be sufficient without reducing client experience? Do you really need to hire a new staff member or can you simply increase the hours of an existing staff member? If you do need another staff member, could you simply rent out a chair on a commission based model?

UTILITY DISCOUNTS

If you've been in business for a couple of years and have never been late with a bill, you can call your utility retailers and point that out and ask for a discount.

You can also do some research and find the cheapest rates and ask them to not only match that price but also to offer you a loyal customer discount. I did this with the telephone, internet and electricity companies and received around 20% discounts on all just for being a reliable, loyal client and asking.

BUY SECOND-HAND

While it's nice to buy fresh, new furniture and items for your salon; in reality buying second-hand in some instances is much better. Salons are always replacing their furniture and equipment and selling them cheaply even though they're still in great condition. When I first started out with my salon, I replaced the old tatty chairs with beautiful second-hand quality chairs from Facebook Marketplace. They were less than a year old, the owner wanted to rebrand and refurnish, and sold the chairs she didn't want for just $100 each... after paying nearly $1000 each for them less than a year before.

FORTY-THREE
SALON SOFTWARE

If you're paying for your salon software, check that the free software options might not be just as good for your needs. Check your point of sale (POS) options out while you're at it if you're paying for a complete POS system. At the very least, contact your existing suppliers and ask if there is any discounts available that might convince you to stay with them.

OPENING LESS HOURS

If you have a slow day regularly each week and it tends to be the same day, for example Monday or Tuesday, consider closing for that day altogether so you don't have to pay staff for that day each week.

Also if you find most clients don't like to book in till after 10am, just bring your junior or reception person in at 9am or whenever you open, and bring the stylists in at 10am. This means you're not paying trained staff to stand around and wait for clients to arrive.

FORTY-FIVE
GET FREE SHIPPING

Ask your sales representative to give you free shipping. This can save you a LOT over a year of regular shipping costs. They may have a system where if you order a certain amount, you get free shipping; so make your ordering system more efficient (your salon software should be able to help with this by tracking your records). For example, if you receive free shipping for orders over $1000, then check your tracking records for products that you'll definitely use in the near future to get your order up to that point.

However, if you've been a good regular client, the company will want to retain you and may waive all shipping costs regardless of the amount of your order.

REDUCING RENT

If you're just starting out in a salon or are currently in a slump, talk to your landlord about a temporary rent reduction. It's cheaper for the landlord to do this than risk losing a good steady tenant who looks after the property, and have to spend money on advertising for a new tenant while receiving no rent.

FORTY-SEVEN
EXCHANGE PRODUCTS

To save money on your next product order, ask the sales representative if they'll offer a switch out service on your products that haven't sold at all or been used at all in the past few months.

Sales representatives are generally happy to switch out unopened, unused products for more products that will get used or sold more easily.

INSURANCE COSTS

Insurance for your business can be a killer. Shop around for the best rates and make sure you read the fine print; too many people wait for something to happen to read the fine print.

Consider getting an insurance broker, they can do all the shopping around for you and get you the most competitive insurance rates that will cover your specific needs, saving you hundreds of dollars and tens of hours in research time.

MORE INFORMATION

How do I find out more information, or about other books in the series?

For more great business ideas and books, visit the following links:

https://www.facebook.com/CatherineRBoothAuthor/

https://catherinerbooth.wordpress.com/

Thank you so much for reading with me. If you have questions, you can message me on my Facebook page.

MORE ABOUT THE AUTHOR

Success does not come to those who give up
And now you don't have to.
For most entrepreneurs, the only reason they FEEL the
need to close down their business is because they can't seem
to find the right solution to their problem.
Oh, they tried everything they could think of, but nothing
was able to deliver the results they needed in order to
prosper in business.
.. until they opened themselves up to a new way of thinking.
Creative business solutions are not something everyone
possesses straight away, but it IS something that can be
taught and utilised.
Hi, my name is Catherine R. Booth and I am your creative
business solution strategist.
Nothing would make me happier than sharing my
knowledge, experience and solutions to help you
overcome most any business problem or obstacle –
because creatively overcoming and prospering is what I do
best.
As a multi-passionate entrepreneur, I have worked in so

many different successful businesses, always employing my creative business solutions to enable them to prosper!

One of my favourite experiences though, was buying a run-down business in my local area and turning it into a prospering 6 figure enterprise.

And when I'm not being a creative business solution strategist in my business (and other business ventures), I'm more often than not writing about business and solutions and turning them into published books.

Writing has always been a passion of mine from a young age.

You see, what most people don't realise until they meet me is that I have a wicked sense of humour. Oh, yeah – and I'm deaf.

Did I mention a sense of humour?

But most people don't realise I'm deaf until I speak. Born profoundly deaf, I had to really apply myself in order to develop any form of speech. I also made it a mission of mine to learn how to lip read.

And this is where I get a lot of my creative business solutions from. My starting foundation as a human being was all about needing to be creative, because when you're born deaf in a world of people who can hear – you need to figure out how to not only fit in but stand out!

Which is something both my mum and dad taught me growing up.

My father showed me that nothing is without value. That the broken always bear their scars but their scars make them more beautiful. Things that were once made with love and have fallen apart can be remade again with love – a concept that applies to people, things, nature and business.

My dad never let my deafness define me and encouraged me to use my struggles and obstacles as a way to grow and develop into the best version of myself – and I have carried this lesson with me in every venture I have had.

I went from nursing birds with broken wings back to health as a child to restoring antique furniture and bicycles as a teenager. From that, I moved on to restoring classic cars as an adult which then turned into my passion for restoring and rebuilding businesses in my local community .. businesses that allowed me to help sustain local employment while being able to teach my teams about creative business solutions and prosperity.

While my father taught me to appreciate the art of making broken things more beautiful, my mother taught me the power of valuing and respecting myself and others.

She taught me something so extraordinary that to this day it still plays a role in my success (and hopefully, soon, in yours as well) – she taught me to listen with other than my ears.

How has this taught me to be a successful 6 figure entrepreneur, business owner and author?

When faced with a business problem, often all we can see is what's right in front of us .. and therein does not always lie the solution.

Being deaf, I had to learn how to not only read lips but also take in the body language, facial expressions and the energy of the person all at once in order to really understand what they were saying.

I had to listen with other than my ears .. I had to learn to see beyond the business problem in front of me – hence, I became a master strategist of creative business solutions.

Over the years I have further developed this ability to listen with other than my ears and have invested countless hours in learning human psychology. Going deeper than that, I paid close attention to client AND business owner psychology.

What I have come to know is that psychology and mindset is behind most business problems and obstacles. Yep, you guessed it – we are often the solution to our own problem or obstacle, we just need to learn how to become a creative business solutions strategist.

And this is why I have poured my heart, soul and experience into a collection of short and to the point creative business solution books. Books that focus on overcoming one business problem or obstacle at a time – because busy entrepreneurs don't have time to read and implement full sized books!

I have purposely written my creative business solutions books with the busy and often overwhelmed entrepreneur in mind. As a mother of young challenged children (who are now flourishing adults), I always had a side hustle to keep me interested and our finances robust. I truly do understand time constraints, and needing to manage time effectively while addressing the mindset shift required to develop and grow your business.

I have a big heart for small business owners. I know how hard you work for what is often small reward. Nothing would make me happier then showing you how to creatively overcome obstacles and problems in your business while increasing and maximising your financial and lifestyle rewards.

Success does not come to those who give up...and now you don't have to – learn the art of creative business solutions HERE with me.